BRIGHT
IDEA
BOOKS

FORT KNOX
Protecting the U.S.
Gold Reserves
by Lisa Harkrader

CAPSTONE PRESS
a capstone imprint

Bright Ideas is published by Capstone Press, an imprint of Capstone.
1710 Roe Crest Drive
North Mankato, Minnesota 56003
www.capstonepub.com

Library of Congress Cataloging-in-Publication Data
Names: Harkrader, Lisa, author.
Title: Fort Knox : protecting the U.S. gold reserves / Lisa Harkrader.
Description: North Mankato : Capstone Press, 2020. | Series: High security
  | Includes index. | Audience: Grades 4-6
Identifiers: LCCN 2019029346 (print) | LCCN 2019029347 (ebook) | ISBN
  9781543590623 (hardcover) | ISBN 9781543590630 (ebook)
Subjects: LCSH: Fort Knox (Ky.)—History—Juvenile literature. |
  Gold—Juvenile literature. | Vaults (Strong rooms) —Juvenile literature.
  | Treasure troves—United States—Juvenile literature.
Classification: LCC F459.F59 H37 2020 (print) | LCC F459.F59 (ebook) |
  DDC 976.9/845—dc23
LC record available at https://lccn.loc.gov/2019029346
LC ebook record available at https://lccn.loc.gov/2019029347

Image Credits
Alamy: Jim West, 24; AP Images: cover, 6–7, 12–13, Barry Thumma, 5, 8–9; Library of Congress: Harris & Ewing, 26–27; Newscom: Rick Wilking/Reuters, 21; Rex Features: 23; Shutterstock Images: Janece Flippo, 17, Milica Nistoran, 30–31, RomanR, 18–19, tridland, 14–15, 28, zefart, 11
Design Elements: Shutterstock Images

Editorial Credits
Editor: Charly Haley; Designer: Laura Graphenteen; Production Specialist: Dan Peluso

TABLE OF CONTENTS

CHAPTER 1

A ROOM
Full of Gold

Visitors walked through the door. Guards checked each one. They made sure the visitors did not have anything unsafe. The guards led the visitors to a large safe called a **vault**.

It was September 1974. The visitors were at Fort Knox in Kentucky. The United States keeps gold in the vault at Fort Knox.

A guard stands inside Fort Knox in 1974.

Some Americans were worried. They said the gold was gone. They called the government.

Fort Knox is owned by the U.S. government.

These people were wrong. The government wanted to show the truth. It asked 100 reporters to visit the vault. Ten government officials went too.

The visitors stopped at the vault door. It was made of steel. A guard opened one lock. Another guard opened another lock. They opened the door.

The visitors stared at shiny bars of gold. The bars were stacked from floor to ceiling.

SOLID GOLD

A gold bar is a little smaller than a brick. Each bar weighs about 27 pounds (12 kilograms).

Gold inside the Fort Knox vault in September 1974

CHAPTER 2

BUILDING the Vault

The government wanted to print more money in the 1930s. It needed gold to cover the money's **value**. It got gold from Americans and gave them paper money. Then the country needed a safe place to keep the gold. It built a vault at Fort Knox.

Fort Knox is an army base. It has thousands of soldiers. It is hard to attack. The government made a strong building for the vault.

The U.S. government prints paper dollars.

A fence kept visitors away
from the building in 1937.

ROCK, CONCRETE, AND STEEL

The building was finished in 1936. The outside wall was made of hard rock. Concrete lined the wall.

There was a giant steel vault inside. It was very tall. Its door was 3 feet (91 centimeters) thick. The door weighed more than 20 small cars.

THE GOLD TRAIN

The United States first put gold in Fort Knox in 1937. It was about 368,000 gold bars.

The gold was heavy. The government could not send it by plane. It sent the gold by train. Guards were on the train too. They kept the gold safe.

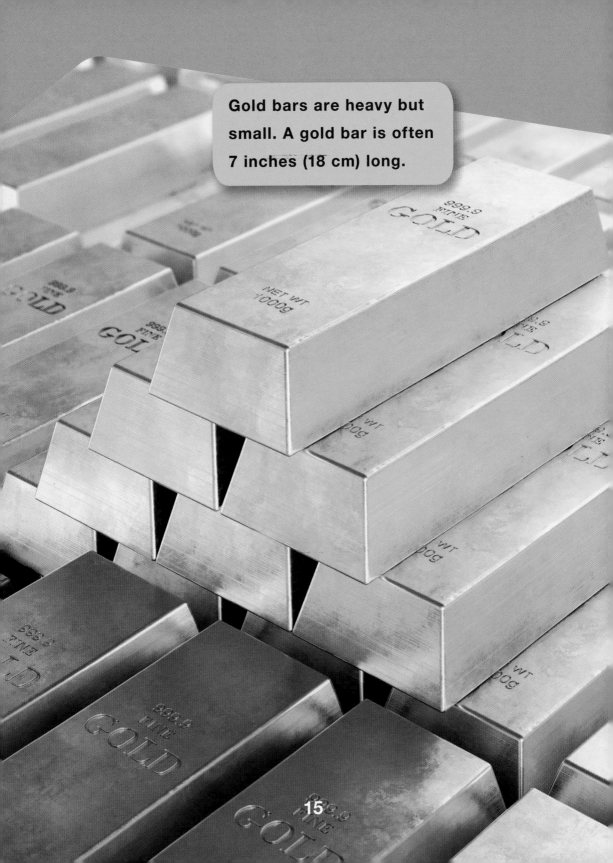

Gold bars are heavy but small. A gold bar is often 7 inches (18 cm) long.

CHAPTER 3

INSIDE
the Vault

World War II started in 1939. Fort Knox protected gold during the war. It protected other things too.

The United States wanted to keep important papers safe. One of these was the Declaration of Independence. Fort Knox held the papers during the war. It also held papers from England. It held jewels from Hungary. It held gold from many countries. The war ended in 1945.

The Declaration of Independence was once held in Fort Knox.

IN CONGRESS, JULY 4, 1776

e unanimous Declaration of the thirteen united States of A

17

Today Fort Knox holds about 5,000 tons of gold. Most is in gold bars. The gold is worth $190 billion.

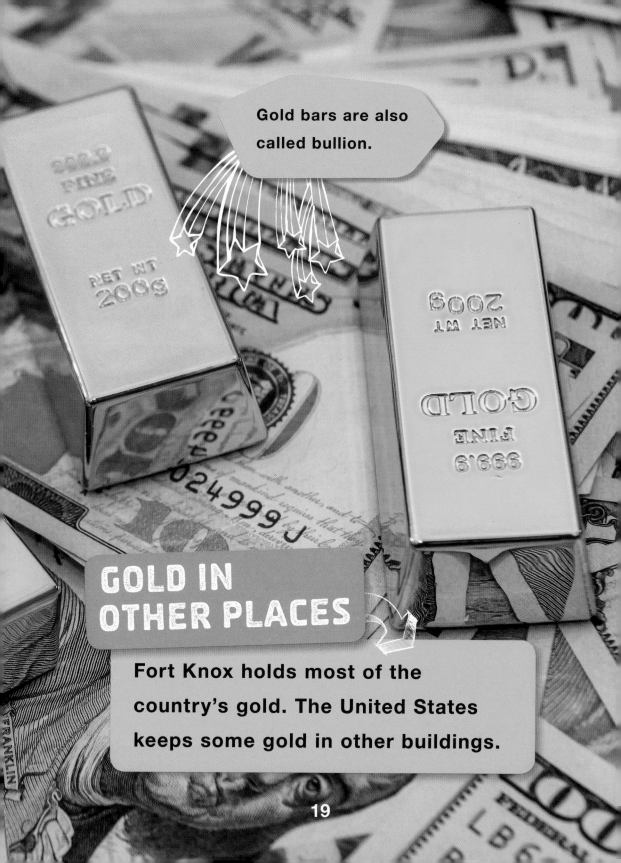

Gold bars are also called bullion.

GOLD IN OTHER PLACES

Fort Knox holds most of the country's gold. The United States keeps some gold in other buildings.

CHAPTER 4

GUARDING
the Gold

Sometimes people say something is as safe as Fort Knox. They mean it is completely safe. Fort Knox is one of the most secure places on Earth.

Fort Knox is very safe because it is an army base.

Fort Knox has three steel fences. It has **electric fences** too. It has cameras.

High-tech devices guard Fort Knox too. The government will not say what those are.

Fences surround Fort Knox.

GUARDS

The U.S. Mint runs the Fort Knox vault. The U.S. Mint Police guard it. The Mint Police is among the oldest police forces in the country. It began in 1792. Mint Police guards train a lot for their jobs.

There are guards at the door to the vault building. Each corner of the building has a tower with guards.

SHOOTING PRACTICE

Fort Knox has a shooting range in the basement. Mint Police guards practice shooting there.

NO VISITORS ALLOWED

Fort Knox almost never allows visitors. Only people who work there can go inside.

Fort Knox has allowed visitors only three times. President Franklin Roosevelt visited in 1943. Reporters saw the gold in 1974. Government officials visited in 2017.

The government works to keep Fort Knox safe. The building is strong. The gold is protected.

GLOSSARY

electric fence
a fence that has electricity running through it, giving an electric shock to any person or animal who touches it

U.S. Mint
part of the U.S. government that makes coins and keeps track of the country's gold

value
how much something is worth

vault
a strongly built room or container with a lock, used to store and protect valuable things

28

TRIVIA

1. Fort Knox has a sealed escape tunnel just in case people get locked inside.

2. Workers have been writing on the concrete walls of the vault since Fort Knox was built. They use chalk to sign their names and write messages. The walls are covered with scribbles and drawings.

3. It takes more than one person to open the Fort Knox vault. Each person knows some of the steps to open it.

ACTIVITY

YOU GUARD THE GOLD

The U.S. Mint takes many steps to secure the gold at Fort Knox. What if you were in charge of the gold? How would you keep it safe?

First think about where you would keep the gold. What place on Earth would be the most secure? Would it be on land, at sea, or somewhere else? What kind of building would keep the gold safe?

Then think about how you would protect the place. Who would guard the gold? What security systems and high-tech devices would be needed?

Draw the place where you would keep the gold. Include all of your security features. Describe how each feature would keep your gold safe. You can add a map to show where this place is located.

FURTHER RESOURCES

Want to learn more about Fork Knox?
Check out these resources:

Cernak, Linda. *Guarding Fort Knox*. Mankato, Minn.: Child's World, 2016.

U.S. Mint: Fort Knox Fun Facts
https://www.usmint.gov/about/mint-tours-facilities/fort-knox-fun-facts

Wonderopolis: Where Is Fort Knox?
https://wonderopolis.org/wonder/where-is-fort-knox

Interested in reading more about the U.S. Mint?
Check out these resources:

U.S. Mint for Kids: https://www.usmint.gov/learn/kids

Vox, Everett. *The U.S. Mint: The History of U.S. Money*. New York: PowerKids
    Press, 2018.

INDEX